Federalsburg Elementary School
302 S. University Ave.
Federalsburg, MD 21632
410-754-9054

For Andrea,
who shared every step of this book
and who made our Milan adventure possible
— J.F.

To the people of Italy, with gratitude for
all they've given to the rest of us
— H.T.

G. P. PUTNAM'S SONS

LEONARDO'S HORSE

Jean Fritz

Illustrated by **Hudson Talbott**

ANYONE who watched the young Leonardo wander the countryside around his home in Vinci might have guessed that he would be an artist. He stopped to examine everything. He looked at the landscape as if he were memorizing it. So it was no surprise when his father took him as a young teenager to Florence to study art.

People noticed that Leonardo was different.

He dressed differently. While other young men wore long togas, Leonardo wore short, rose-colored velvet togas.

He wrote differently. Backwards. From the right side of the paper to the left. A person would have to use a mirror to read his writing.

And he wouldn't eat meat. He liked animals too much to eat anything that had once been alive. Nor could he stand the sight of caged birds. If he saw a man selling birds, he would buy them all. Then he would open the cages and watch the birds fly away. What a flurry they made! How did they do it? All his life Leonardo tried to discover their secret of flying so he could make a flying machine for himself.

For a man who liked to ask questions, Leonardo da Vinci was born at the right time—April 15, 1452. Everybody was asking questions then. The age was called the Renaissance, a time of rebirth when people who had forgotten how to be curious became curious again. They were exploring new countries, discovering, inventing, looking at old things in new ways. What was the point, Leonardo asked, in copying what had already been done? He had to bring his own experience into whatever he painted. You wouldn't catch him putting a halo around the head of a saint. How could he? He had never seen a halo.

Leonardo da Vinci turned out to be a famous artist; still, he was not just an artist. He could never be just one thing. He was an engineer, an architect, a musician, a philosopher, an astronomer. Once he fashioned a special kind of flute made of silver in the shape of a horse's head. The ruler of Florence, Lorenzo de' Medici, asked him to deliver it as a gift to the duke of Milan. This was lucky for Leonardo. He had heard that the duke of Milan wanted to honor his father with a bronze horse in front of his palace. And Leonardo wanted to be the one to make it.

This would be his mark on history. Hundreds of years later people would point to the horse. "Leonardo made that," they would say.

Temporary bridge

Eight-gun cannon

Armored tank

So he wrote to the duke, listing all the things that he could do. He could make cannon, lightweight bridges, and covered chariots that couldn't be broken or harmed. On and on he went, but he saved the most important point for the last. He could make a bronze horse. In the end, he didn't send the letter. He simply left for Milan. Never mind that he was in the midst of painting a large religious picture in Florence. Let someone else finish it. He had planned the picture and that was the important part.

War chariot

Exploding cannonballs

Cannon

Parachute

Catapult

Leonardo was thirty years old now, handsome with curly blond hair. The duke gave him the job of working on the horse, but at the same time he was expected to take charge of entertainment in the palace. He had a beautiful singing voice, he could play musical instruments, he could juggle and ask riddles, and he was also asked to stage elaborate plays for special occasions. Whenever he had a chance, he went back to the horse.

He visited the stables, studying how a horse was put together.

He needed to understand everything about his subject. He measured and drew pictures until he knew where all the bones and muscles of a horse were. But you couldn't show all the muscles on a statue, he said, or the horse would look like a bag of turnips. You should show only those muscles the horse was using or getting ready to use.

He visited statues of horses. Many were shown in an amble—left front leg moving at the same time as the left back leg. This was not easy for a horse; he had to be taught to do it. Leonardo saw one horse, however, that he described as free—left front leg and right back leg moving together, in a trot. Moreover, both ears were pointed forward. (Some horses pointed one ear back to hear the rider's orders.)

Leonardo was ready to begin.

But the duke wasn't quite ready. He wanted a much bigger horse than the one he had originally planned. One three times larger than life. Could Leonardo manage anything that large? the duke wondered. He wrote to Lorenzo, asking him to recommend someone who could do the job.

Lorenzo replied: Leonardo da Vinci was the only one.

On April 23, 1490, Leonardo wrote in his notebook: "I resumed work on the horse." The hardest part would be the casting. He collected 58,000 pounds of metal—tin and copper—which would be heated until it was fluid. This would be turned into bronze and used to cast the horse. But should he pour the bronze all at once? No one had tried a single pouring of anything this large.

In November 1493, he had completed the clay model — twenty-four feet high.

It was shown off at one of the duke's special occasions, and it was a sensation.

But Leonardo seemed to be in no hurry to start casting. Perhaps he wasn't sure how he'd do it. Besides, he was planning a new project. He had been commissioned to cover the wall of a convent with a picture of Jesus and his disciples at the Last Supper. Since he wanted to present the disciples realistically, each with his own personality, Leonardo walked the streets of Milan, looking for the right faces. He had trouble with Judas. He could never find anyone in Milan who looked evil enough. So he left Judas for someone else to do.

Later, in 1498, there were rumors that the French were preparing to invade Milan, and the duke wanted to be ready. And there was all the metal that Leonardo had collected. Just what the duke needed. So he sent it off to be made into cannon. Well, this is war, Leonardo reasoned. What else could they do?

When the French came in 1499, Leonardo and the duke fled. But the horse couldn't leave. There he was when the French arrived. The archers laughed. Never would they find as perfect a target, they said. Pulling back the strings on their bows, they let their arrows fly. Ping! Ping! Ping! The horse sagged. Ping!

Then it rained. And the horse became smaller and smaller.

At last it was nothing but a pile of mud stuck with arrows.

Leonardo went back to inventing and painting, but he never forgot his horse.

He still wanted to invent a flying machine. But he still couldn't do it.

His greatest disappointment, however, was his horse.

As Leonardo became older, his hair turned white and grew down to his shoulders. His beard reached to his waist.

And he became depressed. What had he achieved? he asked himself. He complained to his notebook: "Tell me," he asked, "if anything has been achieved by me. Tell me. Tell me." It was especially hard when his rival, Michelangelo, taunted him.

"You," Michelangelo said, "who made a model of a horse you could never cast in bronze and which you gave up, to your shame."

In his notebook Leonardo mourned, "I have wasted my hours."

On May 2, 1519, Leonardo da Vinci died. It was said that even on his deathbed, Leonardo wept for his horse.

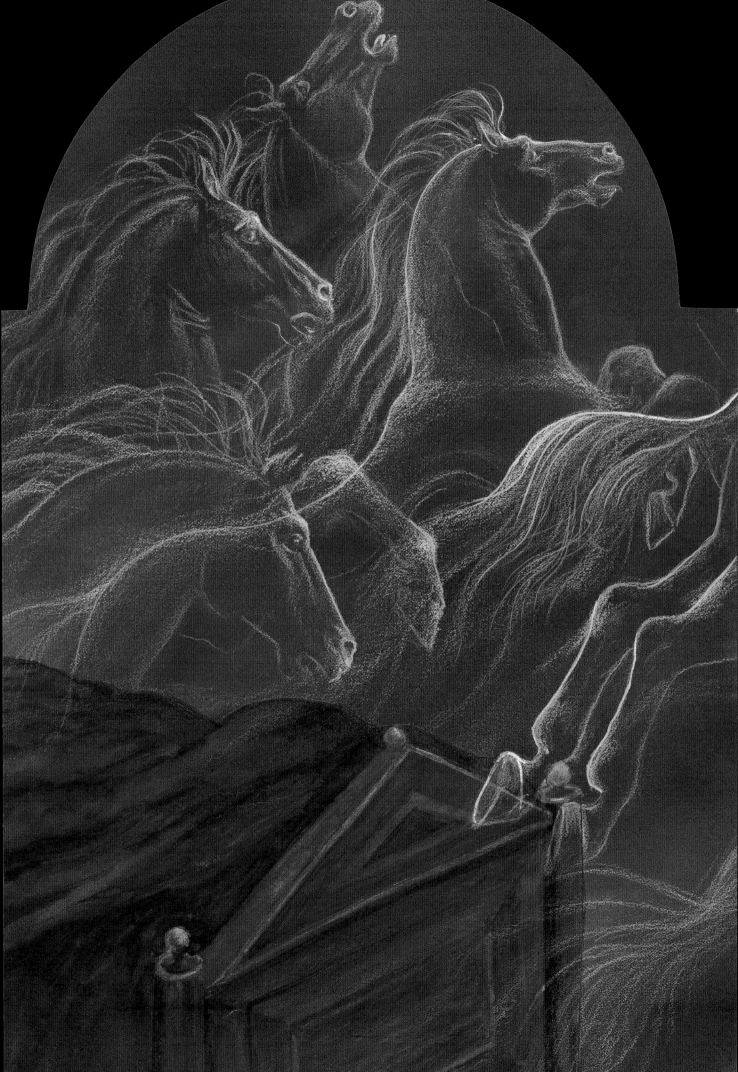

LEONARDO has been remembered for hundreds of years, especially for his paintings *Mona Lisa* and *The Last Supper*. But not for his horse. That story was almost forgotten until 1977, when it was told in a magazine. And the right man read it. His name was Charles Dent. And Charlie loved art — reading about it, making it, looking at it, collecting it. Leonardo would have liked Charlie. They were both dreamers with big dreams. Yet Leonardo may have been envious. Charlie did what Leonardo had always longed to do. He flew, soaring through the sky like a bird freed from its cage. Charlie was an airline pilot, and whenever he traveled, he looked for art to take home.

The more Charlie read about Leonardo and his horse, the more he cared about Leonardo. When he read that Leonardo died still grieving for his horse, Charlie couldn't stand it. Right then he had the biggest dream of his life.

"Let's give Leonardo his horse," he said. It would be a gift from the American people to the people of Italy.

But could he really give Leonardo his horse? Could anyone? Charlie went to see famous scholars who had specialized in the study of Leonardo. When he came home, Charlie was smiling; he could go ahead.

But where would he build his horse? He needed a special building, he decided—a round building shaped like a dome, tall enough for a horse. On top there would be windows to let in the light.

Charlie didn't know a thing about domes, but luckily he found a man who did. When at last the Dome was finished, Charlie hung the pictures he had collected on the walls and arranged other art objects around the room.

All that was needed was the horse.

Every day Charlie could see the horse more clearly. Wherever he went, he carried a small piece of wax or a piece of clay and made miniature models of the horse. But he needed to be around real horses. He borrowed two champion Morgan horses and studied them for months, running his hands over their bodies so he could feel where the muscles and bones were. He measured every inch of the horses just as Leonardo would have done.

Then, in 1988, he began the eight-foot model of the horse. Over the wooden skeleton, he applied one thousand pounds of clay. To hold the horse steady, a post ran through the belly of the horse to the ground. To fill the belly, the horse was stuffed with slats of wood and Styrofoam. So now the Dome had a clay horse—his left foreleg raised and bent, his right rear leg off the ground. Free. The muscles in his hindquarters were tense, his ears pointed forward, his nostrils were beginning to flare.

By 1993 the eight-foot plaster model of the clay horse was completed and ready to be cast into a twenty-four-foot bronze horse.

For that it would have to be sent to a foundry where it could be enlarged; a twenty-four-foot clay model sculpted; then the twenty-four-foot bronze horse cast.

In 1994, however, the people at the Dome were less concerned about the horse than they were worried about Charlie. He became sick and no one knew what was the matter. Then he was told that he had Lou Gehrig's disease and it could not be cured. He would not be alive when the horse arrived in Milan. All Charlie said was what he always said: He had never been interested in taking credit for the horse; the gift of the horse was a gesture of friendship from the American people to the Italian people, a salute across the centuries to Leonardo.

On December 13, Charlie's family and friends gathered around his bedside and promised him that the horse would be finished.

On Christmas morning 1994, Charlie died.

On August 1, 1995, the horse was ready to go to the foundry. He was hoisted into a van, tied, padded, and driven off for his great adventure.

At the Tallix Foundry in Beacon, New York, his transformation began. He was enlarged and cut up into sixty separate pieces. They were laid against the wall of the foundry while the Dome people gathered to watch the pieces being put together. It was certainly a huge horse, but was it as grand as Charlie had envisioned?

The Dome friends walked quietly around the horse. They seemed uneasy.

The horse wasn't right.

Art experts were called in. They shook their heads.

No, the horse wasn't right.

He looked awkward. Out of proportion. One of his rear legs appeared to be short. His eyes were not exactly parallel. He needed help.

Fortunately, a talented sculptor from New York City, Nina Akamu, agreed to try to fix him. But when she went to work on the twenty-four-foot horse, she found that the cementlike plaster that covered him resisted change. No matter how hard she tried, she couldn't fix him.

Everyone recognized that there was only one thing to do, but it took a while for anyone to say it out loud. Yet it had to be said. Nina would have to start from scratch and make another horse. For some, the idea of doing away with Charlie's horse was almost more than they could bear, yet they all knew that Charlie would want his horse to be as perfect as possible.

The horse would always be Charlie's dream, but as soon as Nina went to work, he had to become her horse, too. She had studied in Italy for eleven years. Her favorite Renaissance artist was Verrochio, Leonardo's teacher. It was lucky that she was there to carry on with Charlie's dream.

First Nina made an eight-foot clay horse. From it a second eight-foot horse was made of plaster. Using the plaster model as a guide, a twenty-four-foot horse was made in clay.

Everyone went to work to get the horse exactly right. Finally he was ready to be cast in bronze.

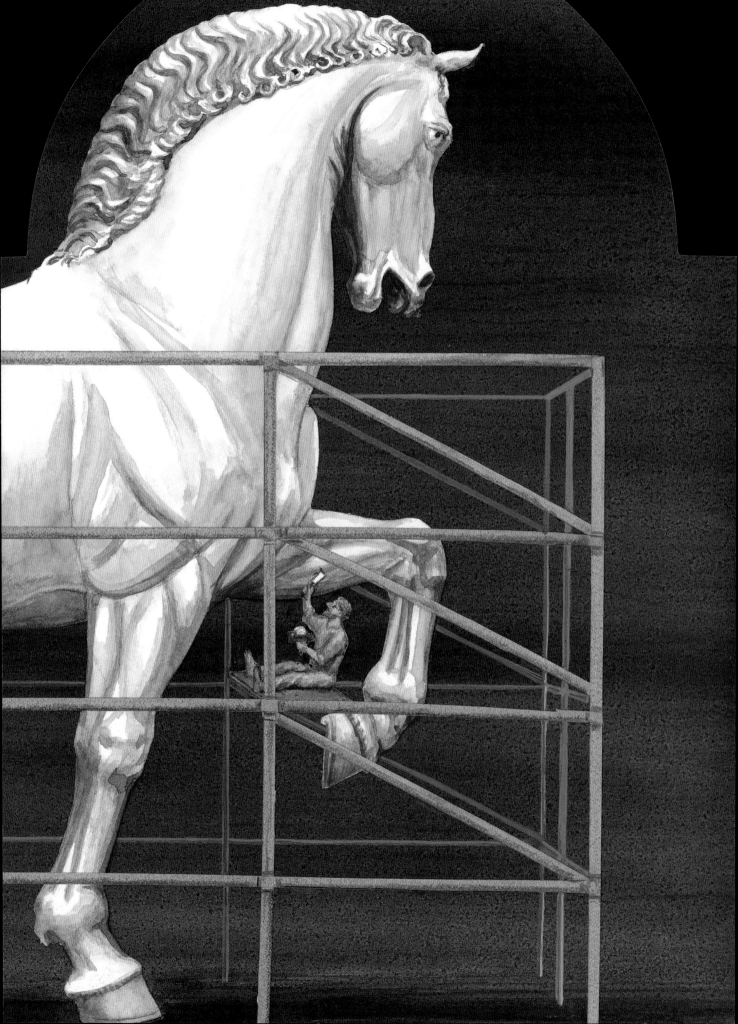

FROM CLAY—TO PLASTER—TO BRONZE

8. The box was closed again and molten bronze was poured through a hole in the top to fill the impression left by the plaster mold.

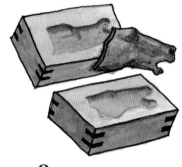

9. After the bronze cooled, the box was opened and out came a bronze piece in the exact shape of the plaster mold.

7. When the mixture hardened, the box was opened and the mold removed.

6. The top and bottom of a box were filled with a mixture of sand and cement. The mold was pressed firmly into the bottom, and the top closed, encasing the mold in the mixture.

10. One by one the bronze pieces were welded together, and the horse began to take shape.

1. Thin metal pieces called shims were stuck in the clay to divide the horse into sections.

5. Each section hardened into a plaster mold.

4. . . . then filled with plaster.

2. Liquid rubber was sprayed onto the horse to make the molds.

3. Each rubber-coated section was removed . . .

But how could such a large bronze sculpture stand on two legs? First they built a steel skeleton inside the body of the horse to support the sides, and then they inserted steel tubes in the two legs. The tubes were bolted to steel anchor plates below the hooves and embedded in concrete.

Finally, the horse was complete. Everyone stood back and looked up at him. They agreed that he was ready for his new home.

If Leonardo had finished his horse, he would only have had to move it from the vineyard where he worked to the front of the duke's palace. Charlie's horse had to cross the ocean to Italy. But he was too big.

So he was cut up into separate pieces, crated, and flown to Milan, where the Tallix people and the Dome people waited to reassemble him. Workers would crawl through a trapdoor in the horse's belly to fasten the pieces together.

He would stand on a pedestal in a small park in front of Milan's famous racetrack, within whinnying distance of the racing stable.

On June 27, 1999, the horse took off.

September 10, 1999, was the date set for the unveiling of the statue,
exactly five hundred years to the day since the French invaded Milan and
destroyed Leonardo's horse.

An enormous cloth was spread over the horse so he couldn't be seen. Two
huge clusters of blue and white balloons were attached to either end of the
cloth. On the pupil of one eye of the horse, Nina had written in tiny letters
Leonardo da Vinci. On the other eye she had written *Charles Dent*. She had put
her own name in the curly mane of the horse.

As a large crowd of Italians and Americans took their seats, the horse stayed in hiding. Speeches were made. The Italian national anthem was sung. Then the American national anthem.

Finally, the strings anchoring the balloons were cut and the cloth rose into the sky.

Ahhhhhhh!

At last Leonardo's horse was home.

ACKNOWLEDGEMENTS

In his will, Charles Dent left almost everything to the horse. At the same time, people from all over the country were sending gifts to help with the work of finishing the horse. It took many people and a great number of donations to make this possible. Thanks go to all these people.

And special acknowledgement is made to those people who took over Charlie's work and saw it to completion. Listed below are the names of the original board of trustees, along with names of new members. The activities of Leonardo da Vinci's Horse, Inc., will be continued so that more people can appreciate Leonardo's world.

AUTHOR'S NOTE

Charlie had planned to paint the finished horse gold, just as Leonardo had expected to do. But the people of Milan said they already had one gold statue in the city. That was enough. So gold was ruled out.

When the twenty-four-foot horse was completed it was possible to make others, but the Board of Trustees decided to allow only one more to be made. This would be an American horse. Frederik Meijer, one of the most enthusiastic and generous of the original donors, bought the American horse and placed it in the public gardens he had already donated to the city of Grand Rapids, Michigan, where he lives.

For more information on the activities of Leonardo da Vinci's Horse, Inc.:

Leonardo da Vinci's Horse, Inc.

Sovereign Building

609 Hamilton Street

Allentown, PA 18101

www.leonardoshorse.org

Text copyright © 2001 by Jean Fritz. Illustrations copyright © 2001 by Hudson Talbott. All rights reserved.

This book, or parts thereof, may not be reproduced in any form without permission in writing from the publisher, G. P. Putnam's Sons, a division of Penguin Putnam Books for Young Readers, 345 Hudson Street, New York, NY 10014.

G. P. Putnam's Sons, Reg. U.S. Pat. & Tm. Off. Published simultaneously in Canada.

Manufactured in China by South China Printing Co. Ltd.

Conceptual design by Hudson Talbott. Typography by Cecilia Yung and Gunta Alexander.

Lettering by David Gatti. Text set in Cochin.

The art was done in watercolors, pen and ink, colored pencil, and collage.

Library of Congress Cataloging-in-Publication Data   Fritz, Jean. Leonardo's horse / Jean Fritz ; illustrated by Hudson Talbott.   p.   cm.   1. Cavallo di Leonardo (Milan, Italy)—Juvenile literature. 2. Bronzes, American—Juvenile literature. 3. Bronzes—20th century—United States—Juvenile literature. 4. Horses in art—Juvenile literature. 5. Dent, Charles C.—Juvenile literature. 6. Statues—Italy—Milan—Juvenile literature. 7. Leonardo, da Vinci, 1452–1519. Francesco Sforza—Juvenile literature. [1. Leonardo's horse (Milan, Italy). 2. Horses in art. 3. Dent, Charles C.] I. Talbott, Hudson, ill. II. Title.   NB1230 .F75 2001   730'.92—dc21   00-041550   ISBN 0-399-23576-0

7 9 10 8 6

JEAN FRITZ

first learned of Leonardo's and Charles Dent's dreams of creating this horse in 1999. She read of the pending shipment of the sculpture from the Tallix Foundry to Milan and went to see it the weekend before it left. The magnificent horse and its story captivated Jean.

"This horse belongs in a picture book," she told Peter Dent.

And so it began. Her research took her to Charlie's Dome in Pennsylvania as well as the spectacular unveiling of the horse in Milan (you can see her in Hudson Talbott's painting of that scene if you look hard enough).

Winner of a Newbery Honor for her autobiographical book *Homesick*, Jean has written over thirty-five highly acclaimed books for young readers, including *And Then What Happened, Paul Revere?*, *Will You Sign Here, John Hancock?*, and *Shh! We're Writing the Constitution!* for younger readers, and *Bully for You, Teddy Roosevelt*, *Why Not, Lafayette?*, and *You Want Women to Vote, Lizzie Stanton?* for middle-graders. She is considered the top biographer writing for children and young people today. Jean lives in Dobbs Ferry, New York.

HUDSON TALBOTT

grew up in Kentucky, surrounded by horses, and studied art in Italy, where he walked the streets studying faces and buildings just as Leonardo did. He has been enthralled with Italian culture ever since. Once, on a layover at Milan's airport, Hudson planned to visit the huge statue of Leonardo's horse, but ran out of time. He returned home to find a phone message querying his interest in doing this book. He did get the opportunity to return to Milan and visit the statue as research for this book.

Hudson has written and illustrated over a dozen books, including *Forging Freedom*, the dramatic account of how one man's heroic acts saved 406 lives during the Holocaust; *O'Sullivan Stew*, a lighthearted spoof of Irish storytelling; *Tales of King Arthur*, a series based on the Arthurian legends; and *We're Back! A Dinosaur's Story*, which was produced as a feature-length animated film by Steven Spielberg. He lives in New York City. Learn more about Hudson at www.hudsontalbott.com.